In the garden

M000297568

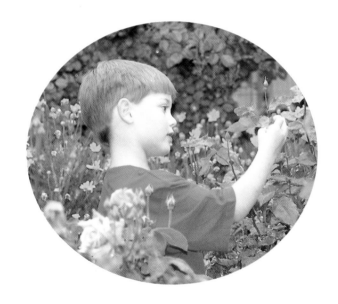

Look at the butterfly.

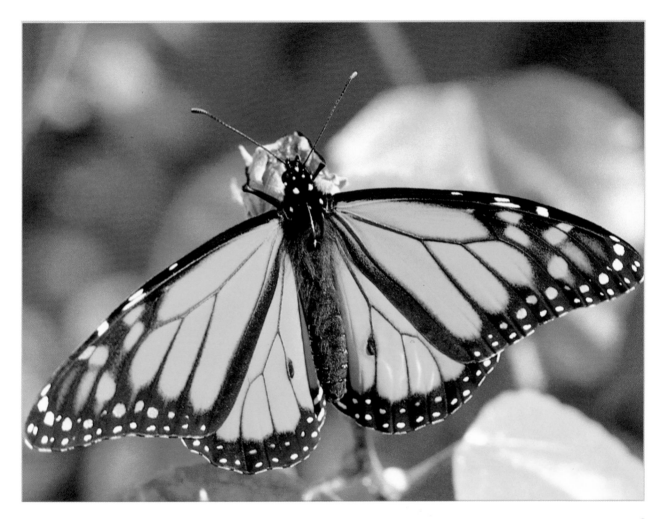

Look at the caterpillar.

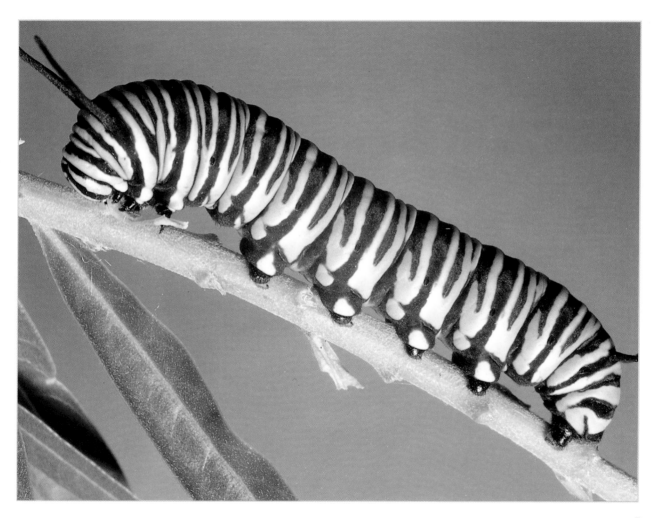

Look at the spider.

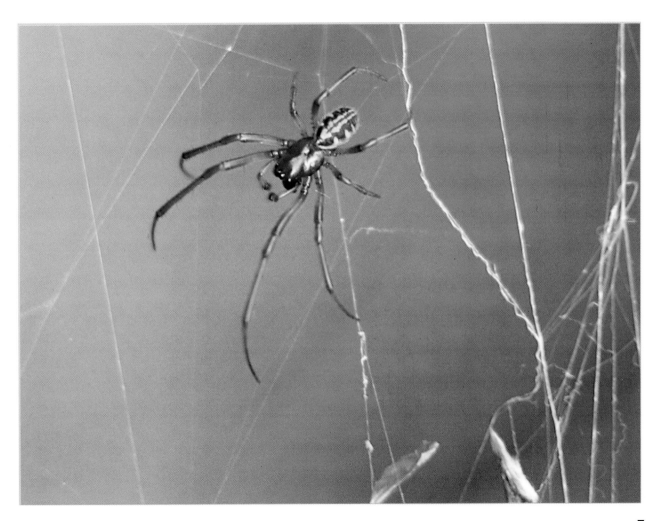

Look at the beetle.

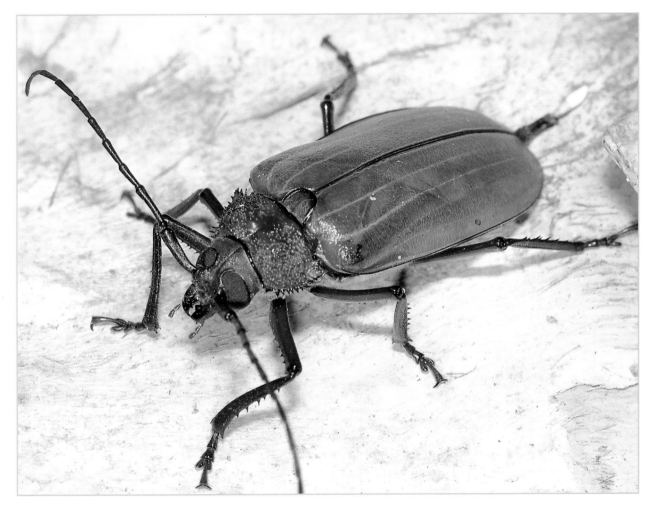

Look at the grasshopper.

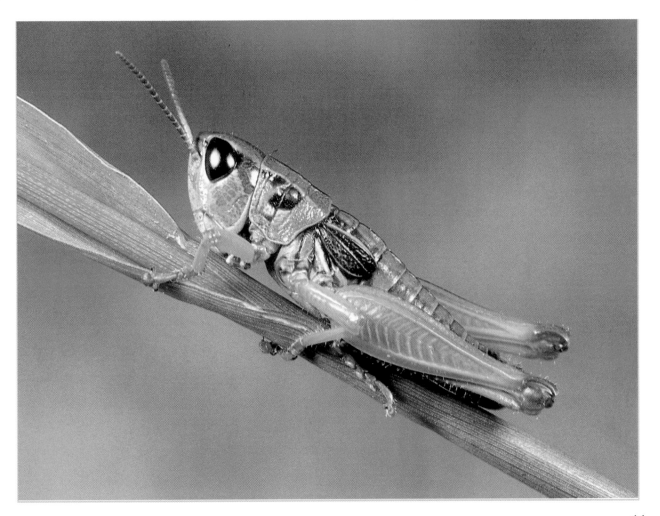

Look at the snail.

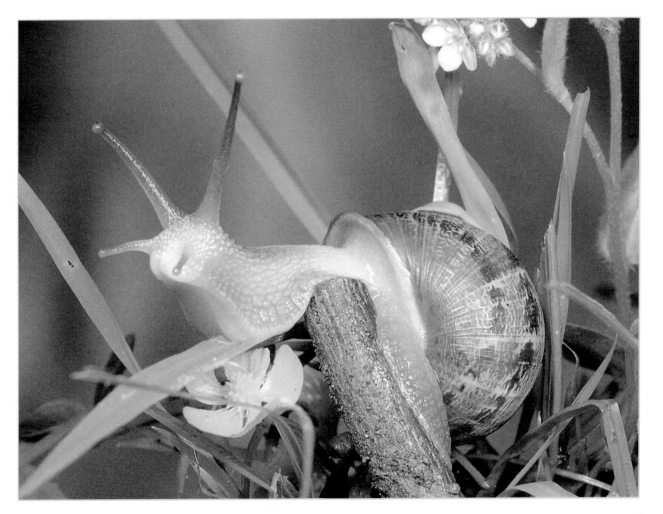

Look at the worm.

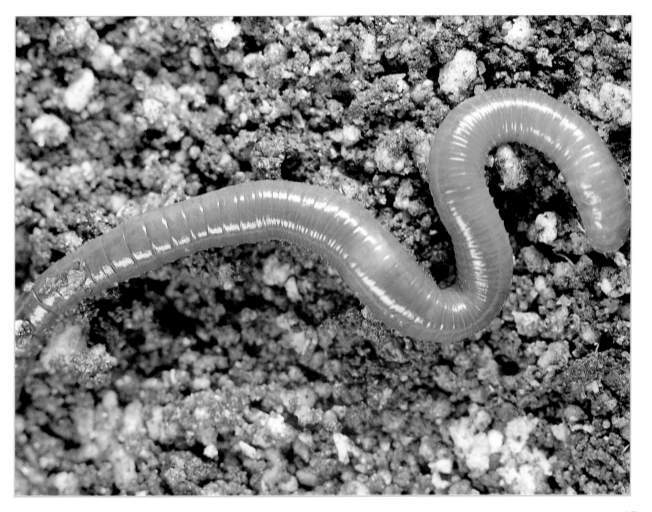

Look at the bird.

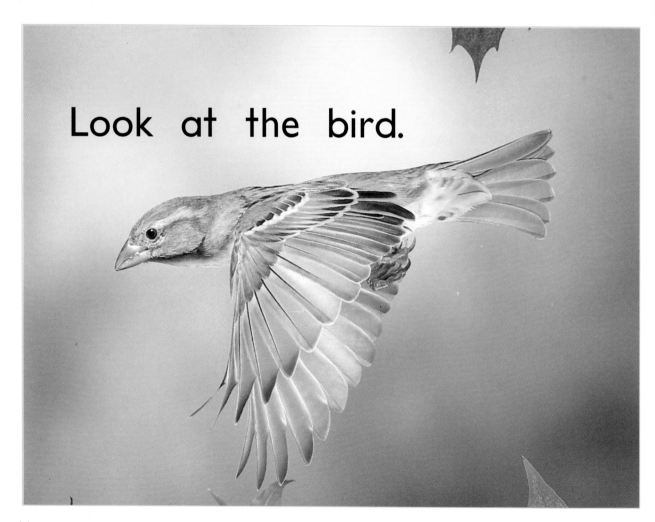